ENOUGH IS ENOUGH!

A Ten Step Program To Bring Black America

From

Dream to Reality

By Rev. Michael Hurndon M.Ed.

Table of Contents

1. Fifty years after the dream.   Pages 1 -5

2. Step one: A refusal to pay taxes

3. Step two: Total refusal to serve in the military

4. Step three: Massive reduction of the purchase of consumer goods.

5. Step four: A truly segregated community.

6. Step five: Death before disrespect

7. Step six: Repairing the black family.

8. Step seven: From arrogance to repentance

9. Step eight: The Payment of Reparations

10. Step nine: A life for a life

11. Step ten : The refusal to ever be a nigger again

Fifty years after the dream.

On a clear day in 1963 a dreamer stood before of a crowd of 250,000 people to declare his vision for future generations of African Americans. America and the world listened intently as he defined a Nation that would become far better than it was and is, a Nation that would not judge a man by the color of his skin but by the content of his character. Many in the crowd envisioned a repentant nation that would come to grips with its sins against an innocent people, pay for its murders committed on the middle passage and insure that the description declared on the pages of the U.S. Constitution, that all men are created equal, would become more, much more the than empty platitudes.

On that day in 1963 black people as a whole were trapped in poverty, forced to reside in segregated communities and shut out of the economic life of America. At that time the school systems failed to provide an equal quality education for children of color. At that time we either volunteered or were forced through the draft to lay down our lives in Vietnam for a nation that failed to offer us full inclusion.

We sought to confront these injustices by taking part in a civil rights movement. We marched all over the south and north, peacefully asking an evil government to set aside centuries of bigotry and social discrimination and do the right thing by its citizens of color.

During the Johnson administration, civil right legislation became the law of the land. These weak laws had no real strength and even the creation of government offices to enforce them have not made any dramatic changes. And so even in 2015 Blacks continue to experience on a national scale, community segregation, employment discrimination, lack luster community resources and an atmosphere of non-inclusion.

(1)

Fifty years after the dream

Today if you desire to seek out the poorest portion of any American city you need only inquire of a resident to give you directions to the black part of town. Fifty years after the dreamer declared his dream, the majority of blacks still live in the American nightmare. Fifty years later the schools of America are still segregated and Black children are still denied equal educational opportunities. Fifty years later and employment discrimination still traps black families in a cycle of dire poverty. Fifty years later and we still fight the battles for a Nation that provides the false appearance of Justice while at the same time permits the reality of lackluster representation to persist. Fifty years later and Blacks are still the last hired and the first fired. Fifty years later and Blacks as a whole still struggle to earn a living in a land plenty.   Fifty years later and our unemployment rates are almost double that of whites. Fifty years later and our representation in the prison population far exceeds our percentage of the general population. If you place a man in the cage of economic impoverishment, if you steel from him even a glimmer of hope that his despair is temporal, if you display as a Nation a genuine distain for justice and rob him of his name, his identity and self-worth, it should not be shocking that he conducts himself as an animal. The hypocrisy of America is shown in its creation of a massive problem and its finger pointing at the victims of its blinding cruelty as well as its declaration that somehow the victim is responsible for his own deplorable condition.

The White Man's history has demonstrated that he is blinded to the needs of people different than himself, that he is governed by greed without compassion, that he is greatly limited in his

(2)

Fifty years after the dream

ability to take responsibility for his historical and present day crimes, that he is confident of his

racial superiority, though his actions put him on a level with the beast. From the acquittal of

Police Officers who shoot unarmed black children, to judges who hand out longer sentences to

blacks for the commission of the same crimes as whites, to government efforts to end affirmative

action policies, it is abundantly clear that this Devil will not reform his ways without unyielding

force. Just as a Tiger will not deter its attack because you blow him a kiss nor will a venomous

snake turn from its prey because you offer a hung and forgiveness, the White Man will not

change his ways and repent because we march, sing spiritual songs or tolerate his abusive

behavior for another day. We as black people must become unified in our determination to bring

an end to the White Man's arrogance in this country, we must become non-supportive of a bias

nation and demand that this country create true equal representation under the law or no longer

remain active participants in its operational structure.

This book is not another publication that suggest that we beg Caesar for our due. We have tried

the tools of passive resistance, we have strove to gain justice through the courts and patiently

awaited for a nation to repent. In general our cries have gone unheeded and our warnings of

impending social disaster have been scuffed at.

As the Author of this text, I would like to join the voices of millions and declare that enough is

enough. This book seeks to offer a strong and unyielding plan of attack in a real revolution that

demands social as well as economic change for the disenfranchised segment of the population.

If we conduct a historical examination of the contents inherent in an authentic revolution we

would soon be forced to concluded that there was never a revolution that did not cause human

Fifty years after the dream

suffering, self-sacrifice and bloodshed. The Civil Right revolution of the 1960's attempted to defeat an unrelenting foe using the tools of passive resistance, Christian principles of love and forgiveness and an unbridled faith in America's ability to heal herself. Fifty years later it should be evident that this country is either unwilling or unable to do this on any significant scale.

We must remove ourselves from the victim mentality and stop patiently waiting for America to do the right thing. America will not and cannot make appropriate and significant changes without a revolution. Black members of this society must start now to change the way we think. We must confront Americanism in the same manner as we would defend ourselves against a physical aggressor. Malcolm X once declared that we must achieve our righteous objectives by any means necessary, these words are still as current today as when they were first uttered by this Black Revolutionary.

No revolution can hope to be successful without a strong, structured and precise battle plan. This book attempts to suggest such a plan. To the reader these ideas may appear to be strange at first glance, perhaps even insane. This is not surprising due in part to the fact that many revolutions seem crazy at there inception, even the so called American Revolution. I have no illusions about the fact that many examiners of the strategies presented here will be in total disagreement with the solutions offered but my recommendations are founded on the history of white behavior both past and present. I offer these ideas as only as starting point to a larger mass movement of the minority population.

Enough is Enough! No more employment discrimination.

(4)

Fifty years after the dream

Enough is Enough! No more segregated school systems and lackluster educational opportunities. Enough is Enough! No more killing of our sons and daughters without consequences or race retaliation. Enough is Enough, No more massive impoverishment exclusive to the black community. Enough is Enough ! we refuse from this day forward to submit to your mental abuse, your racism, your arrogance, your stiff necked refusal to truly repent and pay for your crimes against humanity and your undaunted refusal to get your foot the hell off our necks.

Step one: A refusal to pay taxes

In the Bible we are told that Jesus said render to Caesar the things that be Caesars and to God the things that be Gods. This scripture implies in an offhanded way that the collection of taxes is a justifiable reality and obligation of the population. I am convinced that the Bible has been tampered with by whites to fit their agenda and justify their actions. Within the pages of the scriptures we also find the words, "slaves obey your masters". Can a righteous God really instruct his faithful followers to obey a human master. Would a creator who truly loves and cares for his children really direct them to submit to mental, spiritual and physical abuse. I know beyond a shadow of a doubt that the Creator has our best interest at heart and he wants and has always wanted us to serve only him as our master. Only a devilish minded people would think of themselves as equal with and deserving of the same adoration as God.

The American Revolution began with the logical foundation that a people should not be obligated to pay taxes to a system that did not fully represent that people's interest. This is known as taxation without representation. The colonist went to war, the cost in terms of human life was massive and yet today there actions are glorified and admired. Why is this so? And if it is correct and responsible for whites to refuse to pay taxes to a system that did not have their best interest at heart or a genuine concern for their wellbeing, what justification is there for the paying of taxes by Americas ex-slaves.

When you pay Taxes to a system of government you are providing the revenue required to keep that government in operation.

Step One: A refusal to pay taxes

When you pay taxes you are declaring in a tangible way that you desire that a system of government be able to continue to function and accomplish it primary agenda.

What does an intellectual examination of the statistical realities reveal about the primary objectives inherent in the American political structure. Are the policies created and enforced by the United States designed to lift Blacks out of horrific poverty, do they sincerely seek to structure a national environment that is conducive to equality and lasting change? The answer is not difficult to discover and the numbers in all areas of American life reveal the truth. The answer is a resounding No!

Our presents and participation in the life of this Nation is documented as being here even before the American Revolution. History reveals that the first person to shed his blood for the liberty of this country was a black man, Crispus Attucks who died on March 5, 1790 as a casualty of the Boston Massacre.

This nation became one of the wealthiest nations in the world off of the back of a free labor market. Today America continues to make policies that under educate blacks and create an impoverished class in order to provide a cheap workforce to keep its capitalist machine operational.

We must stop paying into America's genocidal agenda of black economic destruction. Just as history reveals that white people refused to buy into a system that did not fully represent them at the start of this country, we must also demonstrate that we are an equally intelligent people and reject taxation without equal representation.

Step one: A refusal to pay taxes

If we want to be respected as a people we must stop paying the devil for our own annihilation.

What can America really do to force all of her ex-slaves to pay taxes. I suggest that the only thing that they can do is to create a truly just system and pay for their crimes of murder for white profit or remove us from the tax roles. We must accept no less than what he demands from a government that he buys into, equal representation under the law.

For those who are self-employed stop sending in your tax forms today and shout from the roof tops, that enough is enough! Demand that this nation respect our future generations by aggressively refusing to pay for anything less. For those who are employed by others refuse to pay a penny more than what is deducted from your checks and mark on your tax statement that you are exempt. If blacks must remain exempt from equal employment opportunity, if we must remain exempt from police protection but continue to be the victims of unchecked police brutality, if the value of black life must remain less than that of white life and if the 3/5 clause of the constitution must stay intact, then we as an entire people must refuse to buy a defective product.

The brutality of slavery and the millions of lives stolen because of it must never be forgiven and such a crime must be paid for in total. Just as the future generations of blacks continue to be the recipients of the "nigger mentality" beaten into the slave and just as whites continue to benefit in every area of American life in relation to their whiteness, they must be made to see that they have also inherited the unspeakable crimes of their past generations.

When blacks refuse to pay taxes to this American flawed system and wholly disconnect ourselves from its tax system we will force this government to seriously examine its destructive policies.   (8)

Step one: A refusal to pay taxes

The white man has been able to manipulate people of color all over the world through a policy of divide and conquer. The time is now that we become a united people and a nation within a nation that no longer ask for but demands equal representation and protection under the law.

Black people take a closer look at where you live and where the bulk of white people reside. In black neighborhoods do you receive the same quality services as the whites, are your sidewalks maintained as well, are your schools as modern and well equipped, do the police respond as fast when you are a victim of crime and are your interest taken to heart by the local political leadership. It has been said that you get what you pay for. The time is now that we stop paying for the bigotry of America.

Yesterday while in a local restaurant buying a sandwich, I mentioned to a friend the recent tragedy of a black man that was put to death. A police officer applied a choke hold to the neck of his unarmed victim while attempting to arrest him for selling single cigarettes. The police officer was later acquitted of any wrong doing. One of the white male customers interrupted our conversation and aggressively declared that we should, "shut up and stop whining!" about this horrific murder. I let him know how sad it is that he is continuing to breath and therefore just wasting Gods good air. His attitude is an example of the evil heart of white people who excuse the violence imposed on blacks. This evil heart is entwined not only in the bulk of the white population but also within the politicians who have no problem spending our taxes in the form of their salaries.

If we return an eye and eye, putting one of their sons or daughters in a choke hold for the commission of a misdemeanor, would these devils still remain so emotionless and cruel.

Step Two: Total refusal to serve in the Military:

A key ingredient of a strong nation is that nation's ability to defend herself. American is not only an economic might all over the world but also a military power to be reckoned with. We as blacks in America are large part of the military strength of this broken nation. Black youth join the military in massive numbers due in part to excessively limited economic opportunities in areas where they resided. Few genuine opportunities in their community turned what was supposed to be defined as a volunteer service into a no other options reality. Since the nations involvement in the Iraq war minority numbers have dropped off slightly. As of 2010 blacks in the military service numbered 2.4 million. Our numbers continue to be extremely low in positions of high leadership. (Generals)

The very fact that many of our young people feel that they have no other choice but to join the armed forces if they want to be successful, is the clearest indication as to why we as a people should not be represented. Any area where large populations of blacks reside in the United States is absent of good industrial jobs and even have few service oriented positions. Our young have lost hope at having a fair chance to attain the American dream from the very start of entering the work world. Black families who are already struggling to survive on often meager wages are pressured by impoverishment to sacrifice their sons and daughter to the American war machine. The very environment that maintains our exclusion is also instrumental in forcing us to defend its continuation.

We must end the insanity of participating in a military designed to defend a country that will

Step Two: Total refusal to serve in the Military:

not stand up to defend our right to be members of the human family.

The same Senators and Congressmen who cash the pay checks that come from the pockets of struggling black people stand for legislation to end affirmative action policies and limit our voting rights.

How can we continue to face bullets to defend the white man's power structure and at the same time tremble when it comes to defending our own liberty and changing the reality of our future generations. It is the mission of the American military to defend to the death the American way of life. A life that has been a death trap for the majority of blacks since its very inception. Only a fool would fight to the death to defend his enemy's right to destroy him. Only a people devoid of even a reasonable amount of intellect would risk life and limb to keep this brutal capitalist regime in power in order that they may continue in their arrogance.

We must refused to serve in this nation's military. We must have enough respect for ourselves to refuse to lay down our lives for the beast that would rob our children of hope and destroy their souls. The American white power structure has put a price tag on the value of our children's lives and determined them to be worthless or at least worth less that our white counterparts.

Throughout European domination of North America, whites have clearly demonstrated that they have a respect for any people that will insist that they be respected and will enforce that insistence by violence if such actions are warranted.

We need only examine the Japanese Americans and how they were treated just a few years after being place in Interment Camps in this country.

(11)

Step Two: Total refusal to serve in the Military:

During World War II and directly after the attack on Pearl Harbor, because Americans feared that the Japanese would turn on them from the inside, Japanese citizens were removed from their homes and place in camps, many for the duration of the war. In the 1980's America provided a heartfelt apology for these actions and gave Japanese Americans along with their descendants reparations in the form of twenty thousand dollars. This was payment for less than four years of unjustified imprisonment.

 Black people have suffered under brutal white capitalism for over four hundred years. We were not only removed from our land and property but robbed of our history, our name and our recognition that we were members of the human family. We suffered and continued to suffer as a community within a larger community, separated intentionally from the pecuniary opulence of a nation that displays no hint of remorse for its transgressions. *In recent decades the US Government has conceded that their behavior toward blacks, was both morally and ethically unjustified and even a crime against humanity. The government has said, "Sorry about that", as payment for four hundred years of murders, rapes, beatings, kidnappings, lynching's and robberies. With the same voice used to apologize they state that this is no way implies that reparations will be paid.*

 What a nation of hypocrites! Can you or I stand before the court of justice and declare our guilt, say I am sorry and walk out of the court room confident that our verbal declaration is sufficient to heal the victims of our actions. Reparations is not a handout nor an entitlement program but rather one small part of the penalty for a crime so massive in its scale that it can't be appropriately measured by human intuition.

(12)

Step Two: Total refusal to serve in the Military:

The commitment that blacks have displayed in the past in connection with military service has prolonged the time when America will sincerely repent for her crimes against an innocent people. We must begin now to develop a determined refusal to sacrifice our sons and daughters to European democracy. A democracy that so far has only offered us the crumbs of freedom and a pretense at justice.

We must be of the mindset to only exchange are willingness to serve this country when they have shown beyond any shadow of a doubt that they are willing serve our best interest.

If blacks feel that they must serve in a military cause, let us create our own army. Let us find a way to finance our brightest and strongest young people to defend our own independence. A people will never gain respect by fighting the battles of others and ignoring their own needs. What have we genuinely profited by sacrificing our sons and daughter to the gods of white capitalism? After our fathers have sacrificed their lives on smoky battle fields on foreign lands, our unarmed children are shot down like dogs in the street. We as a people are refused justice in the courts of this land and white Grand Juries permit the guilty to walk free. Would white society make excuses if a vile Criminal Justice system were murdering their next generation. Would they declare business as usual if the Gestapo practices of police departments throughout this nation were slaughtering their youth.

(13)

Step three: Massive Reduction of the Purchase of Consumer Goods.

Why are there so few jobs in black communities? How is it possible that we are one of the nations biggest consumers of disposable products and yet statistically the poorest segment of the population? How is it that we have missed what was revealed by the Montgomery Bus Boycott and failed to apply it nationwide?

When Rosa Parks refused to give up her seat to a white man on a city bus in 1955, she set in motion a movement that demanded immediate change in America. The bus company wanted the fares of their black passengers and came to realize that if they were to have them they had to treat their customers as equals. The walls of Jim Crow began to fall.

The key reason why there are so few jobs in traditionally black communities is because very few of the dollars that we spend are reinvested in areas where we reside.

One of the things that I discovered when I was a self-employed salesman in the city of Chicago is that white people send their money where they live. When they work in our communities they arrive in our areas with bag lunches, they don't even support the eating establishment in the area. I remember trying to sell a white man working in our community an umbrella during a terrible storm, I even dropped my price to cost but he preferred to get soak and wet rather than spend a dime away from home.

We as blacks cannot see the long term benefits of shopping with our own, in our

(14)

Step three: Massive Reduction of the Purchase of Consumer Goods.

neighborhoods. Yes, we may have to spend a few pennies more in black owned businesses because they are normally charge more for their inventory but we keep the resources where we live, creating employment development and expansion of opportunity.

We shop in stores that have failed to created jobs where we live, that refuse to provide equal opportunity across the board when it comes to black promotion and that have very few black managers. The Montgomery Bus Boycott should have shown us the importance of refusing to buy anything less than absolute equivalency. We need to begin now to investigate as well as question the regular hiring practices of places where we shop. Does our favorite store employ any black managers, what is its percentage of minority full time workers and how does it compare with our national population rates. We must stop sending our capital with those who fail to have our best economic interest at heart. If these stores want our business then they must employ blacks at fairer percentage rates. We must ask owners at what rate they employ blacks and if it is clear they employ few blacks, tell them about our dissatisfaction and take our business to their competitor. When corporations remove their factories from where we live they must come to understand that they have also cut themselves off from our dollars.

(15)

Step three: Massive Reduction of the Purchase of Consumer Goods.

America has always been a place that is dominated by the satisfaction of personal greed. The present capitalist system, as it presently exist in the USA is not only the economic enemy of blacks but also of poor whites. The continuation of racism as an unspoken national policy has insured the impoverishment of the masses. The average white persons implied superiority comes at a very high price. This mental suggestion that they are somehow better than the struggling people of color all around them has given implied justification to the one percent of Americans that dominate its financial landscape.

We as black people in this country hold a truly untapped power that lays dormant in our purses, our pockets and our bank accounts. The dollars that we spend in America and where we spend those dollars hold our destiny. We must keep as much of those dollars in areas where we live by any means necessary. A dollar spent or denied in the right location can mean the difference in rather our sons and daughters get the jobs and economic opportunities that they are entitled to.

As mentioned earlier, I worked in my own business for more than fifteen years and in all that time I never took one single black dollar spent with me for granted. Each of those dollars helped me to provide for my family. I recall repeatedly addressing my customers as Ma'am and Sir. I remember several time being asked why I did this by my customers and explaining that they were helping me to be self-supporting, it was an honor to provide a product for them and that I had a clear awareness that they could have brought that merchandise from anywhere and from anyone other than myself.

(16)

Step three: Massive Reduction of the Purchase of Consumer Goods.

Black business owners must become committed to not taking black dollars for granted but giving quality service and respect to each individual. It must become evident to them that their growth is a key ingredient to real, "black power," in the minority community. When black consumers become keenly aware of the connection between money spent and minority prosperity this must not decrease but increase the quality of service provided to them.

The leadership within our community churches must stop being permitted to rob their members though superstition and tradition. The Church, which is one of the strongest institutions in minority communities, must become equally motivated to save both the man and the soul. The justification of its collection of massive capital must be displayed by its investment from the pew to the pulpit of a determined outward environment that promotes as well as encourages financial strength through capital investment on every level. We have heard enough of the entertaining sermons that make no lasting changes, we must demand that Pastors act as Jesus did. Jesus feed both the body and the soul. Let black people work together to close down churches that make Pastors wealthy behind the walls of churches that do little to nothing in transform the monetary realities of where we reside.

The time is long past when we as a people can support a policy of business as usual in response to the violence that goes unchecked among our people and to our people. It should be clear to the most meager of intellectuals that this social structure was never formulated to benefit the minority population but in the creation of a deliberately plotted genocidal agenda.

(17)

Step Four: A Truly Segregated Community

Saint Paul shares these prophetic words in Romans the 12th Chapter and the 2nd verse, And be not conformed to this world but be ye transformed by the renewing of your mind, that you may prove what is that good, and acceptable , and perfect will of God.

The Apostle Paul shares a very prophetic word here on how we should define our relationship not only in connection with this finite planet on which we reside but also on how we can mentally evaluate our standing within this national community called America.

"And be not conformed to this world". We as black people in America have displayed a conformist attitude that often boggles the imagination. To conform means to fully comply with the rules, standards and laws of a governmental body regardless to the overall justification of its policies. A conformist acts and accepts societal behavior with little to no questioning on the correctness and moral righteousness of the regulations and practices. For the conformist the law is God, legislation is correct because it exist and rules should not be designed for man but man should get with the program regardless of what that program offers. Equality, compassion, an offer of human dignity and ethical principles all play second fiddle to the Jehovah's of Government. If an individual is a conformist it is highly unlikely that that person will join in a revolution to overthrow an unjust government, instead such a person will argue with the inactive millions who aggressively declare that it is best to keep things as they are.

18

Step Four: A Truly Segregated Community

We as members of the so called black community have traditionally been conformist. We patiently await our turn for laws to become divine edicts and political leadership to create legal writings that imitate moral scriptures. We are conformist because killing our kids is not enough to simmer our declaration that we are Americans, We are conformist because the providing of an unequal education does squash our fear and reverence for big brothers tax system. We are conformist because we sacrifice our sons and our daughters to the Lords of capitalism, we pray for the continuation of a pretense at democracy. We are conformist because if you kick us we will remain on the ground just so that we can be a part of a failed experiment. If you spit on us we will and have continued to wipe off the spittle while pledging allegiance to a pack of vicious dogs. I pledge allegiance to the United States of America!

 When a people conform and submit to an unrighteous system of government they permit those who hold leadership positions in that government to continue to fail to fulfil one its key responsibilities, that of protecting the weak, the widow, the children, the poor and all those that cannot protect themselves. A real democracy does not seek to abuse and neglect the few in order to overwhelmingly benefit the many. Real democracy is not so entangled with the trappings of capitalism that it places a strangle hold on the dreams of youth and creates an atmosphere where hope becomes nothing more than an empty promise, by the shackles of hopelessness. For the bulk of young minorities present day societal norms forces them to be unwilling participates in the creation of their own nightmares. Enough is Enough, We have conformed for too long and submitted our very souls to a nation that has neither conscious nor compassion.

(19)

Step Four: A Truly Segregated Community

The historical Jesus was not a conformist but a revolutionary. The bible presents a messiah that was in direct conflict with both the political structure and the religious elite of his day.

The Roman government was concerned about this iconic figure that rose up among the common people to offer a genuine alternative to a government of domination. A government that excessively taxed its captives and dehumanized those it viewed as subordinate.

The black Israelites had become a hopeless people under this system of brutalization and were looking in desperation for the promise of a new kingdom, a kingdom governed by justice and equality and a kingdom of true liberation.

This Jesus talk of bureaucracy coupled with benevolence and administration tied up with the cords of empathy presented a challenge for the tyrannical Roman regime. This Jesus offered sight to the blind, healing to sick bodies and minds and freedom to those held by physical and spiritual captivity.

Just like today, this created a problem for a state without direction from the undeniable divine deity and politics absent of acquiescence or contrition. The creator of every good thing declares that his people should come out from among them and his son introduces a new form of God inspired government.

The ecclesiastical authorities also had a problem with this Jesus. The message of Jesus challenged the status-qua and compelled each religious leader to examine personal motives as well as determine whether his commitment to traditionalism outweighed his desire to grasp a genuine relationship. The church had become a part of the problem rather than a solution. The church leadership were hypocrites because they preached a message of an absolute being while at same time instilling fear in the people of an autocratic state.

(20)

Step Four: A Truly Segregated Community

God cannot move on behalf of black people in America as long as we insist on conforming to a social order that is bent on our destruction. Black people continue to call on God to act in our best interest and to avenge our ancestors as well as present and future generations from a nation of policy makers that instill suffering without justification and it seems that our petitions have always fallen on deaf ears.

May I suggest that the problem is not the slowness of Gods response but the possibility that we are praying to the wrong God. The character of God does not change, he is the alpha and omega, the beginning and the end, the first and the last. The bible presents a God of enormous patients, love and compassion. We also learn that God moves quickly to respond to his suffering faithful. He showed up without delay to rescue three Hebrew boys in the mist of a burning fiery furnace and Daniel's lion's den experience demonstrated that his power is absolute. So why then has God not brought America to her knees for her sins? The bible records that we have not because we ask not or we ask amiss. We as blacks in this wilderness of North America must stop asking God for full inclusion, stop seeking the peace and tranquility of a nation built on the bloodshed and bodies of kidnapped Africans. Let us come to understand that the real God of both heaven and earth is a God of peace but also a God of Justice. The real God avenges the murder of the innocent and brings to repentance both individuals and nations that will not give credence to his power or are the enemies of his chosen people. Let us pray not for inclusion but independence. Let us pray not for conformity but for the creator's supreme justice. When we petition as a people, the real God and when our prayers line up with his character and personality, history reveals that we will be heard.

(21)

Step Four: A Truly Segregated Community

Romans 12-2 : but be ye transformed by the renewing of your mind

This section of the chosen scripture reveals that a change in attitude from conformity requires a transformation into a renewed mind, a new form of thinking.

The first step black people must take in the creation of a truly segregated community is an entirely new way of thinking and evaluating our place in the American economy and the American culture. Creating our own sovereign community requires that we direct the future of our own survival, that we create our own jobs, businesses and services. It is of vital consequence that we have absolute control over the distribution of black currency and that

it is used to benefit us first before in aids the community at large. A strong and vibrant economic community is

respected in a capitalist environment and compels aggressive investment by corporations.

  I am convinced that it would help blacks to examine and evaluate other minority communities in large American

cities and discover how they are structured. When we do such an examination we would discover that such

communities function by providing employment for their own first and that if businesses desire to operate within

these neighborhoods they are require to offer meaningful employment as well.

  We as blacks must insist that the factories that sell us our shoes, create and manufacture them were we live,

giving our working class families the shot at good paying industrial jobs. Any product that depends on heavy

purchases by blacks must in turn return the favor by reinvesting revenue where it acquires its profits.

We as blacks make tremendous contributions to the American economy through enormous purchases of

consumable goods and service. We can make our communities economically healthy by making sure that the bulk

of our dollars stay at home. Large corporations must get the message that, Enough is Enough! They can no longer

take our dollars for granted.

(22)

Step Four: A Truly Segregated Community

Only those corporations that display a sincere willingness to assist us in our rise from the most impoverished

segment of the populous can expect our loyalty. No income equals no monetary outcome.

  A truly segregated community means that we control law enforcement, we control all public services and we

control all health care facilities where we reside. Before we can hire one white teacher, before we can employ

one white doctor and before we give one white person a job in our own back yard we must hire our own. The white

power structure has done everything possible to insure that equal employment opportunity is either grossly curtailed or non-existent and we must provide for our own before we can assist anyone else regardless of their

racial makeup. A people must be respected when they demonstrate that they possess the intelligence to feed,

shelter and protect their own families and their own kind first. Is it racism for me to refuse to provide additional

opportunities to those who are already given the upper-hand? Since it is clear that equal opportunity is a fallacy

let us also become masters of unequal opportunity, creating a way out of no way for our own.

 Let us insist on a truly segregated community. A community that segregates our economic resources to only

those willing to share the wealth though redistribution. A truly segregated community where our own receive the

advantage of gainful employment. A truly segregated community where black teachers are not required to

instruct our children on the lies connected to American history. Let the truth be told to our children, that white

Americans have historically been a band of thieves, kidnappers, murderers, treaty breakers, rapist and enslavers.

 Let our Teachers tongues be set free to make our next generation aware of the black holocaust imposed on them

by a nation of people that made themselves wealthy by treating blacks as beast of burden for over four hundred

years, without sincere repentance. Enough is Enough! Repent America Repent!

(23)

Step Four: A Truly Segregated Community

 A truly segregated community for blacks in America will transform the way we are perceived by

others, allow for a spirit of economic independence to spread throughout our communities and

strengthen the future for generations to come.

The final part of Romans the 12th Chapter and the 2nd verse records, "that ye may prove what is that good and acceptable and perfect will of God."

 When we as a people step out from our conformist attitudes and become committed and serious about developing a new way of thinking, then Gods perfect will can become a reality in all of our lives. Division and selfishness has benefited the few at the expense of the many.

We will discover; what is that good, perfect and acceptable will of our creator when we allow his will have dominance over our own desires. We will speed up the day when God controls our destiny, when we stop believing that America in interested in solving the horrific issues that are eternally present in the black community. A really strong black community must be centered around uniformity of mind and spirit in order to increase the likelihood of long-term change. A truly segregated black community will create an environment of dependency on each other rather than criminal governmental policies. The good and perfect will of God is that his people be freed up to give him and only him the glory and the praise he so richly deserves.

(24)   Step Five: Death before

Disrespect

On Tuesday January 20th 2009, I watched intently along with millions of Blacks as Barak Obama became the first President of the United States of America. The tears flowed down my cheeks on this historic day as I began to reflect on all the things that I have experienced in my lifetime as a Black in America. I found it to be astonishing and mesmerizing that I had been permitted to live long enough to see an African American elected to the highest office in the land. On that day I thought that perhaps there was a glimmer of hope that the country had finally come to a turning point in its chronological record. I was temporarily convinced that just because the new president in the White House had the same pigmentation as I did; that America was ready to become a truly color blind culture.

I quickly discovered that the ex-slave had once again been hoodwinked, bamboozled and lead astray. It should not be surprising that we were tricked because that's what white people do and centuries of practice have made them experts. Native Americans defined their failed promises as a people that speak with fork tongues. The Fourteenth Amendment to the U.S. Constitution guarantees that all individuals (Blacks) must be treated the same as other individuals in like circumstances. I would like to declare that a law that cannot or that is not able to be enforced is the same thing as having no law at all. What is the effectiveness of fair housing laws when the bulk of African Americans can't afford to reside in the communities that we have been set free to live in? What real power is given to us by the appearance of an equal education, when the academic environment of most blacks is extremely poor? Our black children are murdered not only physically but intellectually as well. Oprah Winfrey shared in a documentary how enormous funds are spent on the education of white children and how their interest in learning is encouraged and generated by a variety of expensive programs designed to help them love their school and the learning process. Black children are treated like criminals at their schools. The programs at black

(25)

Step Five: Death before Disrespect

schools are severely limited, the students are not expected to learn in many schools and resources are grossly limited per student. If a black child strongly desires to learn he is expected to make straw without bricks. Many students in black communities are expected to complete homework assignments without enough books for every child. The message is given to our children early in life that they are expected to fail and there is another group in the community whose education is paramount.

In the black community women are more likely to find gainful employment and be the bread winners of their households. A Black Man regardless of his education, training and back ground is traditionally the last hired and the first fired. The black family is targeted for destruction and we as a people are disrespected in every area of American life. We as a people have been disrespected to the point of disbelief and so many have become no more than the walking dead. How do we set our selves free from the constraints of white hatred and racial injustice? We begin to discover the clear path to mental and physical freedom when we intellectually and spiritually refuse to accept anything that is less. Our attitude must be surrounded by a determined notion that we will either have full respect as members of the human family or we will have death. We must become as other nations and people throughout history who have steadfastly rejected domination in any of its forms. The ideology of death before disrespect does not whimper nor tremble but is concise and focused in its unrelenting objectives.

Imagine the determination of so called patriots such a Patrick Henry who declared give me liberty or give me death. The price tag that is regularly attached to the elusive realities connected with unconditional liberty is the total surrender to that which we hold most dear.

When a people are determined to attain liberty and can clearly define what that liberty looks like, they have

(26)

Step Five: Death before Disrespect

started on the path to being set free from the trappings of colonialism and the false propaganda inherent in European democracy.

As unfortunate as it is, human sacrifice has often been the price tag connected not only to freedom but also to bondage. When our enemies no that there is no sacrifice too great and that we are willing to lay down our very lives on the Alter of Justice, they are compelled through the natural order to respectfully submit.

We as blacks in America have over the centuries granted to our slave masters a power that should only be reserved for the creator of the universe. We do not consider our names as legal names unless they are given America's seal of approval. We have granted America the power to make our marriages legitimate and the Ex-Slave masters have taxed almost every action that we endeavor to perform.

 If we are to be segregated from the economic prosperity of this nation, if are children are to be segregated in the treatment that they experience with the law enforcement community and if segregation remains the unspoken law in every area of the American nightmare except when it comes to the defense of this country. We as blacks must not fear segregation but we must enthusiastically embrace it. We must separate ourselves from a people that have always been a destructive force throughout our history. Segregation is the corner stone of a people's independence. Segregation demands that we rely on our own initiatives in enhancing our future generation's development as a mature contributor to human advancement. We must insist on separation in our professional and personal lives.

In the book of Exodus God did not liberate his chosen people from the bonds of slavery without separating them from the presence of their brutal task masters.

(27)

Step Five: Death before Disrespect

The people had to be separated both psychologically as well as physically. We as Africans in the wilderness of North America must begin now to separate ourselves from this white devil both psychologically and physically. We must demand real freedom, by any means necessary!

Six million so called Jews were able to be thrown into the furnaces of Nazi Germany because they accepted disrespect at greater and greater levels absent of forceful, determined and uncompromising retaliation. A people that will accept national and global disrespect will remain as sheep for the slaughter.

How were these so called Jews lead to their own destruction? They were convinced by their government of their own inferiority. They psychologically participated in their own destruction. They were separated from the economic and cultural life of Germany and failed to quickly devise a separate national agenda. What lessons were learned by the holocaust imposed by the National Socialist Party? A people that will not stand up and insist that they have a legitimate right to exist and govern their own destiny, will be manipulate to the benefit of those that do not have their best interest at heart.

Yesterday while in the bowling alley a young man approached me and asked me what is the significance of the black ball and the white pens in bowling? I declared that I did not know. The young man smiled at me with eyes that indicated that he was about to share a bit of profound information. He excitedly imparted that it is the only time when a black man has the balls to knock the hell out of an assembly of whites.

(28)

Step Six: Repairing the Black family

"And he that stealeth a man , and selleth him, or he be found in his hand, he shall surely be put to death." Exodus 21:16

The penalty for the stealing of a man is made clear in Gods word, such a man should be put to death. This scripture is not a call for revenge but a declaration of the Creators righteous judgement. If an individual should be put to death for the kidnapping of a single person; what should become of a nation of people who performed this very act not for days or months or years but for centuries. America is guilty of the robbery of our names, our history and our heritage.

America still holds the stain of having pull asunder children out of the arms of their loving

mothers and the separation of family members that can never be reconnected.

We who are blacks in America by our very presence attest to the crimes of this unrepentant

nation.

How can we find our identity? How can we rediscover a sense of family and strengthen these

bonds with each other. White America has worked hard to separate us into different factions. The

light skinned blacks are more attractive than those of darker pigmentation, blacks that have

naturally straight hair have "good hair" and a small segment of the black population that has

been welcomed into the economic life of America are somehow better than the struggling

masses. The first step in a successful conquest is to divide and conquer. We as a people have

been conquered through division.

Some might suggest that the plight of black families in America is not at bleak as the so called

prophets of gloom and doom would have us to believe but the reality of the numbers cannot be

ignore or denied.

(29)

Step Six: Repairing the Black family

As of the last census count in 2013 there were 45 million blacks residing in the United States

which is equivalent to 14.1% of the overall population. The USA incarcerates more

of its citizens than any country in the world and blacks make up more than 50% of that

population. African Americans are more likely than any other segment of the population to be searched and arrested after a routine traffic stop. 51% of black men have never been married and 14% of black marriages end in divorce or long term separation. The black family is confronted with extreme economic hardship and additional challenges not faced by the general population.

Black young men just one generation out of Jim Crow lack strong examples in our still primarily segregated communities of the roles and responsibilities of fatherhood. The limited employment opportunities and the tremendous failure of public education to provide equal academic experiences for minorities increase criminal behavior. The black poor are forced to fight over the meager resources available where they live. America has purposefully created a program of genocide that continually seeks to destroy the black family. Drugs that can somehow be controlled in the white community, run rampant in black areas. On almost every block there is a tavern. White society distributes its poisons to a people that have been robbed of their self-worth and kept hostage psychologically, economically and morally. White society has spared no expense to keep the masses of black citizens as a cheap labor force and in doing so has destroy the fabric of what is required to make strong and lasting black families. Our men have been turned into the walking dead as a result of dreams too long deferred and our women have sold out to a capitalism that has placed great value on the external without definition of how to structure the internal.

(30)

Step Six: Repairing the Black family

We as blacks must take the reins now, to escape the destructive plans of the European culture. Family is the key ingredient that provides each community with its identity and values. When we permit families to fail we are permitting ourselves to fail. To strengthen black families we must come to realize in our hearts and minds that every black boy is our son and every black girl is our

daughter. We must become a family of one in this wilderness of North America. When one black

is shot down in the street we must come to believe that we all have lost a family member and that

that life must be avenged. If one child gets trapped by the snares of drug addiction then we as a

family have failed our child. We must not permit white society to use our communities as a

dumping ground for her poisons, enough is enough. The family must destroy every drug house

in our community and every establishment that would endanger the mental, financial and

spiritual growth of the family. We must become a family of one that is unbending and

uncompromising in its determination to heal itself from the black holocaust. Our children must

be well educated and we must not trust our enemies to provide that education. Those of us who

know our history and have excelled scholastically must come to see that our future is bound to

the academic future of each and every member of present and future generations of blacks.

The black community must take on a new definition as one large black family. If one of its

members is harmed then it must be the responsibility of the entire family to demand justice.

I believe that each time an unarmed youth is shoot by a racist police officer and each time a

bias justice system permits the guilty to go free, it increases the likelihood that the value of black

life will not be respected by the masses.

(31)

Step Six: Repairing the Black family

The oneness of the black family, a unit that is uncompromising in its insistence that we are a

strong and determined foe, willing to die if necessary in order to protect our own must become

an actual reality.

If American society refuses to give up her plan for Black Genocide and distribute her wealth evenly among all segments of the population, then the black family must become the rock and the strong hand of self-determination. No innocent black life must be taken without retribution, no youthful black dreams must be denied because of lackluster opportunity and America must be made to pay for its crimes against an innocent people.

We must become uncompromising when it comes to creating future generations of blacks with a soldier mentality. A soldier mentality is a thought process that insist on responding to a survival instinct and a determined awareness of self-preservation. We as a black family unit must surrender the notion that to fully love ourselves is a failure to be patriotic.

We do not owe any form of allegiance to an unrepentant American system that refuses to repent of her past and present sins. It is not racism to love our black skins and hate those that have hated us without a justifiable cause. God himself provides no forgiveness to those who steadfastly refuse to repent and we as a people are not required to provide such foolish pardons.

The black family must experience a fresh spiritual awakening. We must reconnect with the God of our fathers in order to truly escape the demonic trappings of an immoral society. We have been captivated be the devil's capital, falsely comforted by his drugs and alcohol and swayed by sermons in our churches that comfort itchy ears but do nothing to inspire revolution or motive us to demand justice for our children.

(32)

Step Six: Repairing the Black family

It is not racism to learn to love ourselves and hate those who have hated us without a justifiable cause. The time is now that we come together as a unified entity with a clear vision and sound conviction that we as the bloodline of bondsman will form the common purpose of preservation.

The community of the black family must be designed in a format that is unyielding and unrelenting in its affirmation that racial detestation by this abhorrent authority will be demolished. This must be a goal that is aggressively strived after without any form of compromise or capitulation. We have surrendered to the intolerable for far too long and America must come to understand that enough is enough!

(33)

Step Seven: From arrogance to repentance

" Talk no more so exceeding proudly; let not arrogancy come out of your mouth: for the Lord is a God of Knowledge, and by him actions are weighed." 1Samuel 2:3

America, a country that started off as little more than a barren wilderness has grown and prospered to become one of the world's most powerful countries.

America can easily be described as one of the most emulated countries as other

Lands seek to dress American, eat American and look American. The growth of America can only be matched by her arrogance. The United States Flag is known throughout the world as a supposed beacon of freedom but also as an emblem of domination and the unspoken idea that the American way of doing things is the only right way of doing things. America has been and continues to be a destructive force when it comes to its relationships with nations inhabited by people of color.

When American arrogance blocked any possibility that this country would set their captives free and sincerely repent it lead to the bloodiest war in this nation's history. Brother was pitted against brother in a conflict that eventually lead to the lost of over 620,000 lives. Until as recent as the beginning of the twenty first century, more lives were lost in the American Civil War than all of the combined wars in the history of the United States. In the end the price for black freedom was paid for in buckets of blood and still we are not fully free.
(34)

Step Seven: From arrogance to repentance

Many glorified and continue to glorify to this day an era when a wilderness was forged into the wealthiest nation that the world had ever seen off of the back of a free labor market. Slavery was considered a required good and an institution that allowed the superior whites to remove themselves from the drudgery of common labor and focus on intellectual pursuits.

As mentioned earlier, America has verbally apologized for her horrific actions regarding Blacks in America. The words, "We are sorry" are worthless as payment for crimes that stagger the imagination. How can three words make up for Africans being stacked on slave ships, forced to lie in their own feces and chained next dead prisoners for days? How can three words quiet the agonizing moans, heard through the silent winds of history as captives succumb to the ravages of filth and disease? What words can vanquish the memory of hungry sharks following the routes of slave ships, confident that their hunger for human flesh would always be satisfied. See the people that were forced to toil from sun up to way past sun down, without rest or compensation, beaten with the lash without mercy and in the mist of their cries see what value they place on your declaration. Your apology will do nothing to heal the scares that have lasted down through the ages.

Repentance without action nor just compensation is worthless.
(35)
Step Seven: From arrogance to repentance

 Such repentance is like providing someone who is hungry the opportunity to view an appetizing meal but not permitting them to personally consume any of the foods. Such a person remains hungry and unsatisfied. The black community remains hungry and unsatisfied with a nation that says I'm sorry for centuries of hatred, brutality, discrimination and outright murder but refuses to pay fully for her crimes. What nerve does the white man demonstrate when he implies that his admission of guilt should be received as satisfactory compensation for centuries of degradation.

Two out of every ten slaves died during what was known as the middle passage, the ocean journey from freedom to lifetime servitude. Slaves ships with names such as Brotherhood, John the Baptist and even Jesus give evidence to disdainful attitudes. The evidence leaves no doubt that the white man was and still is the most prolific kidnapper on Earth, the most prolific rapist on Earth, the most prolific murderer on Earth and the most undisputed liar on earth. We as intelligent members of the black community must consistently and with every opportunity share our public distain with his apologies without sufficient action. The white man must never be permitted to forget that such empty vindications fall on deaf ears.

(36)

Step Seven: From arrogance to repentance

Each day the American Justice System stands in judgement for the criminal actions perpetrated by blacks. Judges look down their noses at youthful black men and black women as they impose punishments on them for their offenses. Seldom does the Judge take into account the societal ills that have produced much of the negative behavior. I have discovered that employers use zip codes to reject minorities for equal employment opportunities and that laws intended to create unbiased employment have been far easier to pen than to implement.

Capitalism is a system that demands a struggling lower class of working individuals and that assignment has been permanently assigned to the miseducation, misdirected and socially neglected minority populous. The black community has been expected to make bricks without any straw and then ridiculed for having failed to do so. The White Dictators of this brutal regime have displayed that they are devoid of compassion or empathy for the havoc that they caused and also find it extremely challenging to confess that they are the authors of its continuation.

What can we do as members of the African community to elicit pressure on the country to balance the scales of continual injustice? If a man where on fire would he calmly asked those around him to douse the flames? Would such a man

(37)

Step Seven: From arrogance to repentance

consider those in his presence to have no responsibility for providing relief because they declare that they did not ignite the fire.

American society thinks that we should be content that the fire has been quenched somewhat and that we should be grateful for the drops of water that are

insufficient to end the suffering.

We must bring an end to silent agony and give no quarter for the white mans

Guilt. There is no statute of limitations on the murder of millions and this nation

is and will always be responsible for each drop of blood spilt to satisfy her

arrogance. We who are Africans in this wilderness of North America must raise up

our heads and look our enemies directly in their eyes and never permit them to ever

forget that the blood that drips from the hands of their fathers has been inherited by

their sons. Will the Jews of Europe ever let the people of Germany forget the six

million thrown into ovens on the pretense that they were the master race. Will

White America just let it go when it comes to Pearl Harbor or 911. We must be

loud in the Churches, we must shout in the jails, we must scream on the street

corners and in the media, that we will not quietly be the victims of genocide.

(38)

Step Seven: From arrogance to repentance

We must be strong in our declaration that for every young black life snuffed out in

racist anger a white son or daughter must pay the price, then and only then will our

right to exist be respected. The shouts for justice will then be heard above the

arrogance of wickedness.

Step eight: The Payment of Reparations

In previous steps we have attempted to define the nature of America's crime, to examine the permanent psychological damage caused by the input of ideas designed to create negative self-identification, (that we are niggers) and to keep us in an eternal condition of servitude. The crime is easy to define but if justice is to be accomplished, we must be able to identify as well as weigh the measure of responsibility that each segment of the guilty holds. Is the government alone responsible or do all white Americans hold equal guilt? We must also be able to determine what are sufficient payments to balance the scales and who are the exact victims. Have some members of the community suffered to a greater extent than others and therefore due a larger slice of the reparations pie? If America were to pay adequate reparations would it bankrupt the nation and as former Africans should this be taken into consideration as we demand tangible compensation? Are declarations from whites that they never owned slaves or lived in the era of Jim Crow a solid argument for not paying reparations? What form of reparations should be paid? Should blacks be paid with free education in the colleges and universities of the nation? Should every black in America be paid with a government check?

Would payments in land grants make sufficient remunerations? Should America support and sponsor a back to Africa movement for all those who want to leave? Should these people's needs be provided for and if so, for how long?

 Our adversary must not be permitted to define what we want as he did during the civil rights movement. In the 60's we were duped into believing that what we wanted was equality rather than freedom, justice and reparations.

(40)

Step eight: The Payment of Reparations

We were convinced by whites that we wanted to live next door to the people who rapped our grandmothers and we bought into it. We were told that we wanted to attend

white schools that lied to us about the greatness of founding fathers who were

really criminals. We believed that equal employment opportunities, that never

came, would somehow correct centuries of exploitation and riding on the front seat of public transportation would correct back seat citizenship. We believed the

enemies propaganda and we were compensated with laws that cannot be enforced

and the continuation of racial discrimination at every level. Our communities are

still segregated, there is still massive employment discrimination and we still

remain in second class status.

The statistics clearly reveal that a clean cut white male with a high school diploma

even one with a record of incarceration, has a much greater chance at attaining

economic stability than a college educated black male.

Every native born white American is guilty either directly or indirectly for the

condition of the black community. Every white in this country benefits from

having white skin and nature reveals to us that for every positive there is an equal

and opposite negative. In America that white skin insures a better quality life, a

better quality of education and better job prospects.

(41)

Step eight: The Payment of Reparations

My Father, who had no formal academic training and was an extremely gifted

salesman told me that he could never bring himself to assist downtrodden whites

because he was convinced that white skin could have easily opened the doors of

opportunity with minimal effort.

Imagine if Blacks in this country were able to somehow travel back in time to a period before the European slave trade and America's rape of the African Continent, if we were permitted to bring with us modern weapons capable of destroying all those responsible for our plight. I am convinced that white people are so guilty that the only solution possible to clean up the future mess that they would create would be their total destruction. The Native Americans gave a name for the justified mistrust they had for whites, they declared that he speaks with a fork tongue. His words that seem honest on one tooth of the fork are actually manipulations and cleverly costumed fabrications on the other end of the spectrum.

When asking the question who should pay reparations to the so called African American the answer is not difficult to determine. Every European in America is equally responsible for the horror that they designed and this nation itself is guilty for the enslavement and racist policies that they created. White people all over the world prosper from the crimes that their Fathers and Mothers engaged in and it

(42)

Step eight: The Payment of Reparations

falls on them, each and every one of them to pay the debt. In the United States every White person, no matter how young or old, has inherited the debt attached to their birthright and privilege.

Right thinking white people, as few as they are in number in this country and all over the world know that they are indebted to the people of color that they abused for their mutual benefit.

As the Author of this text I am convinced that the question is not so much who owes the debt but rather what form the payment of the debt should take and who should be the legitimate benefactors.

How do merciless culprits provide adequate recompense for centuries of mistreatment? The criminal is not permitted to tell the victim of his crimes, what is proper compensation, or what form that compensation should take.

The first step in determining proper reparations is to determine what exactly has been stolen from black people in America both past and present and how this can be restored.

Black people in America have been robbed of their labor, their citizenship rights, their heritage, their historical name, their psychological self –identification and their self-determination.

(43)

Step eight: The Payment of Reparations

The crime was and is massive in its scope and the payment of reparations must be equally massive. No one form of payment will suffice in healing the internal and external scares that have been seared into the entire being of the black populous.

All can agree that United States has become wealthy off of the back of centuries of free and exploited labor. Part of any genuine form of reparation must include payment for this stolen labor. The lives that were consumed can never be reinstated but this Country can and should pay for the stolen toil. Just as white citizens have benefited from the efforts of past generations it is not unreasonable that stolen Africans should reap the benefits of their kidnapped and manipulated ancestors.

As one form of reparations, the distribution of checks to every so called African American would go a long way toward balancing the scales. In considering the amount each person should receive I do not believe that it is unreasonable for every descendant to receive at a minimum, one million dollars. For those who would suggest that this amount would bankrupt an already economically strapped nation I would like to first remind the reader that this is nothing more than the returning of stolen funds. As blacks in America we cannot permit ourselves the

(44)

Step eight: The Payment of Reparations

luxury of displaying any form of compassion toward a historically compassionless country.

If America can afford to spend billions on space exploration and provide economic assistance to third world nations, then it can afford to pay for its crimes.

Monetary compensation as one form of reparations must never be considered by the African community as a gift or a favor. It is a long overdue first step toward justifiably healing the damage caused and also demonstrates sincere repentance.

No amount of money alone can correct the enormous destructive effects of genocide that America has practiced on people of color. A truly effective reparations plan must seek to correct every area in which damage has been caused and we must never let America believe that she can buy her way out of her sins simply by issuing checks.

The reparations that we as African Americans must not only seek but demand must not only include a portion of the pilfered opulence but also a structured method for healing and repairing centuries of unquestionable hurt.

American Blacks must be re-educated at the expense of the nation.

(45)

Step eight: The Payment of Reparations

We must be taught to understand Africa's contribution to civilization and we must be given assistance in discovering our true family heritage. It is America that spared no effort to erase our names from our genealogical memories and it falls on America to foster the cost of repairing the damage. We must be instructed on the black heroes of Africa and across the planet. Our communities must take on a new mission that focuses on self-improvement and we must turn our attention away from false heroes such as Christopher Columbus and Abraham Lincoln. Christopher Columbus was an explorer who got lost and Abraham Lincoln was a white President whose slow efforts to free the slaves even disappointed the abolitionist of his day. When his infamous, Emancipation Proclamation became law is freed none of the four million slaves held in bondage in the Confederate States.

Reparations must contribute the resources necessary to insure that future generations of blacks be trained in the skills required to affect self–determination. In the past blacks have been trained to be the working class of a capitalist regime and lack the skills for the development of independent economic resources. We must be trained away from a consumer mentality and become producers. We must produce every element required for a self-sufficient, non-dependent black

(46)

Step eight: The Payment of Reparations

community that can survive as well as thrive absent of European involvement.

We have been robbed of this form of education with the intention that our labor be used for the overall benefit of Americanism and in doing so our own growth has been purposefully stifled and ignored. America must pay for her intentional mis-education of blacks and provide every resource required to correct the situation. This is a true step toward sincere repentance and genuine reparations.

Another question that has been ask is, should America support and sponsor a back to Africa movement? Before any logical discussion of this topic it must be made perfectly clear that blacks both past and present have paid with blood for the unquestionable right to citizenship in this nation. We heroically fought on every battlefield from the American Revolution through Desert Storm and this land is our land! For the majority of blacks who wish to remain here it is their hard earned right and they need not apologize to anyone.

For blacks who honestly desire to depart from North America it is also their hard earned right and since America criminally sponsored the journey here it only seems logical that it financially support the return trip. America pulled our ancestors out of structured communities, removed them from their families and defined them as beast of burden.

(47)

Step eight: The Payment of Reparations

America must support colonies in Africa where blacks who desire to regain their native heritage may safely do so. The economic support of these replanted Africans is the total responsibility of America and must be paid for up and until each returning African can be a self-supporting member of their native homeland. This is not a favor that America would be issuing but a consequence of her criminal kidnapping.

In conclusion, America must pay reparations because she must take full responsibility for her criminal acts and repentance without corresponding action is meaningless. If America is to truly be a great nation it cannot be permitted to wash over its foundational structure, it must be made to right its wrongs.

We as blacks in America must never be satisfied until every wrong toward us has been righted and what has been stolen from us is fully returned on each and every level.

(48)

Step nine: A life for a life

Ecclesiastes 8:11 When the sentence for a crime is not quickly carried out, the hearts of the people are filled with schemes to do wrong. (NIV)

Blacks in America have demonstrated enormous patients in connection with receiving justice in this country. America in return has shown how little respect they have for the value of black life. How many times have each of us watched through the media as those who murder and assault blacks are acquitted in the courts? Each time a Police Officer walks free despite a mountain of evidence and each time a white person is found not guilty of killing a black youth our patients is once again strained and tested.

White American history reveals that the only thing that they truly honor is violence. We as blacks in America must bring to an end our endless patients and confidence that this country has within its fiber the capacity to do the right thing.

Our peaceful wails for justice have produced little to no effects. I believe that when we publicly declare our willingness to forgive those who are not in the least sorry for their inhuman conduct, we appear to be foolish. Even the creator of the universe does not pardon those who intentionally fail to sufficiently repent and turn from their wicked ways.

(49)

Step nine: A life for a life

We as humans are not required to offer forgiveness at a level beyond Gods capacity. The question must therefore be asked, what do members of the minority community do in response to courts that fail to give us justice and murderers of our youth that walk free?

The value of a human life can only be compensated for at the expense of another human life. When blacks are murdered and the clearly guilty walk free the stench of this injustice reaches the nostrils of the author of all creation and he righteously demands retribution. God uses human beings to seek out and provide for this justice and when a government is either unwilling or unable to do this, it falls on the people to gain this justice and balance the scales.

As the title of our book declares, enough is enough! We as blacks must gain the courage to put down signs that mean nothing without corresponding actions. Our marches have not stopped the killings and slogans mean nothing to those that cannot hear. Every time we are unjustly killed, we march, we protest and we destroy our own communities. The enemies of justice wait patiently with full confidence that we will blow off some steam and with the passing of time, we will once again, let it go. How they must ridicule us as they read our meaningless propaganda stating, No Justice! No Peace!

(50)

Step nine: A life for a life

The idea is sound, there should be no peace as long as injustice is permitted to rain. Yet white society knows that with the passage of time we will let it go and return to business as usual. Why should a people that will accept less than justice expect to be given justice?

America must be forced to comprehend the enormous value of a single black life.

If America insist on continuing to devalue black life then it must fall on the entire

black community to police and protect itself. White people are not the gods of

justice and they are not the only ones that can determine how it is fairly

implemented. History clearly reveals that they have an inability the make sure that

justice is equally and adequately distributed within every community. When the

punishment for a violation of the law is not quickly carried out it forces those who

are being victimized to discover other avenues to attain vengeance.

We as Blacks in America must demonstrate that we will not trust this country to

demand that citizens respect our right to exist as members of the human family.

We must create our own justice system and design within its scope our own Judges

and Police Officers.

(51)

Step nine: A life for a life

We must keep this system intact until American is completely able to totally create

an unbiased legal organism. When a society is either unwilling or unable to

provide balanced justice for all of its population, it then falls on the denied segment

of that population to protect its own interest.

We as members of the black community we must take into our own hands our own protection. America has created a police department whose primary

function is to insure the protection of the values and morals of the white middle

class. It is the job of this legal system to make sure that the decadence and violence

created by this racist government remains in the communities it was designed to

destroy.

Police Departments as they presently exist in black neighborhoods are not there

to serve and protect. They are there to maintain a Police State and to make sure that

the animalistic behaviors created by a country structured by race hatred and

intentional poverty remains a destructive force exclusive to the minority

community. In fulfilling this function the imprisoning and shooting of our youth is

a major component of its operational structure.

(52)

Step nine: A life for a life

The new slave system is costumed as a prison system within the confines of areas

that provide limited to no opportunities beyond criminal behavior for economic

sustenance. Capitalism demands the acquisition of tangle materials. In the black

community the legal means of gathering such assets has all but vanished. The

people who have robbed us of equal opportunity cannot be entrusted with the wholesale distribution of justice.

When a black life is snuffed out without rhyme or reason the minority community must come to understand that such a life must be paid for in blood. We as the intentionally detached have an overwhelming inherent burden to permit no senseless execution to go unpunished. We as blacks in America must end our fear of killing those who have no fear of killing us. We must use violent retribution as the last form of retaliation but we must not remove it from the table. Only when our enemies are confident that we are willing to defend our lives with bloodshed will they come to fear the commission of their deplorably delinquent conduct. This fact is sad but undeniably factual.

(53)

Step ten: The refusal to ever be a nigger again

In its simplest form the definition of a nigger is an ignorant person. America has labored hard to insure that we remain just that, an ignorant people, a divided community and sleeping soldiers on the path to our own destruction. In this book I have attempted to the very best of my ability to awaken a slumbering giant. I hope that by reading these pages I have stirred within the readers soul the spirit of revolution. That we as a people learn to not fear revolution but to embrace it.

I pray that my attempt to construct a logical battle plan will eventually bring healing to a wounded people, that this text has not fallen on death ears and that it was structured on a foundation of love for God and the people who love him with all of their hearts.

It is not our fault that we have been made ignorant by centuries of intellectual neglect but it is our fault if we insist on remaining trapped in that ignorance.

We have a power that reaches far beyond the scope of our limited imaginations but the creator is able to bring it to the surface.

We must shake off the shackles of niggers and become what we are and always were, a proud people and a mighty nation.

(54)